Praise for IN A CONVENT GARDEN AND OTHER POEMS

"I do not profess to know the mind of the talented Diane Marquart Moore but I do know something of its grasp of the essential, in things both ordinary and extraordinary, from the poems collected in In a Convent Garden and Other Poems. Moore is an intuitive, fiercely intelligent, and contemplative poet who renders each poem with a precision of language that makes her ideas of the metaphysical palpable and clear. Her poems, propelled by still, but spirited narration, captivate. We are taken many places: the convent garden, a fortress on the bluff, No Name Road, the plains of Khuzestan—each place absorbed by Moore through all of her senses then conveyed in sharp but measured detail to her readers, for the purpose of leading us to higher ground. This life, seen by Moore, is never spare or hopeless, which is the true gift of this book. In fact the whole book is an urging to hope. She does not spare us the truth of the 'marrow of bondage' all of humanity shares, but her poems promise freedom. Moore assuredly directs us to an ineffable Source. Grace surmounts the suffering of this world, and we are led into a revelation of holy shimmer that drizzles on dogs and cats, stone angels, and gratefully on us."

—Clare L. Martin, poet and author of *Eating the Heart First*, Press 53.

"*Mystical Forest* ... finds its spiritual rhymes in ... Hildegard, Sarton and Oliver."
—Darrell Bourque, *Megan's Guitar and Other Poems from Acadie*.

"... illuminates ... as though one is entering the mystical purple light of her artistic mother's "fragile dream."
—Isabel Anders, *Miss Marple: Christian Sleuth*; *Becoming Flame*; and *Spinning Straw, Weaving Gold*.

"... with a painter's eye, her evocative poems lead to places that are personal and universal."
—Michael Miller, *Into This World*.

"... sings of friends, family, place, but also of loss, regret, and wonder...."
—Mary Ann Wilson, University of Louisiana, Lafayette.

IN A CONVENT GARDEN AND OTHER POEMS

ALSO BY DIANE MOORE

POETRY:

Mystical Forest
Everything is Blue
Post Cards From Diddy Wah Diddy
Alchemy
Old Ridges
Rising Water
The Holy Present and Farda
Grandma's Good War
Afternoons in Oaxaca (Las Poesias)
The Book of Uncommon Poetry
Counterpoint
Your Chin Doesn't Want to Marry
Soaring
More Crows
Just Passing Through
Moment Seized

YOUNG ADULT:

Martin and the Last Tribe
Martin Finds His Totem
Flood on the Rio Teche
Sophie's Sojourn in Persia
Kajun Kween
Martin's Quest

ADULT FICTION

Redeemed by Blood
Silence Never Betrays
Chant of Death
Goat Man Murder
The Maine Event
Nothing for Free

CHILDREN:
The Beast Beelzebufo
The Cajun Express

NON-FICTION
Iran: In A Persian Market
Their Adventurous Will
Live Oak Gardens
Treasures of Avery Island

IN A CONVENT GARDEN *and* OTHER POEMS

DIANE MARQUART MOORE

SEWANEE, TENNESSEE

Border Press
Po Box 3124
Sewanee, Tennessee 37375
http://www.borderpressbooks.com

ISBN: 978-0-9898641-0-7

Printed in the USA

Cover photograph by Sister Madeleine Mary, CSM

Cover design by Martin W. Romero,
Grandson of author

For Vickie

CONTENTS

I

II

III

I

SISTER MARY ZITA

I.

I missed Sister Mary Zita's Golden Jubilee,
fifty years of a life professed to God
unmoved by pretensions
and ambitions of this world,
sent to us from a monastic order
in Sagada, The Philippines.

She ran an orphanage and a guest house,
planted a garden wherever she was planted,
baked bread, made marmalade jam in L.A.,
now attends to flowers on St. Mary's altar,
and we wonder where she learned
the art of flower arrangement
that makes the Madonna smile.

Now, she sits, cap snug on a head
that once carried dung cakes for gardening,
wearing a lilac sock with white stars,
looking like an ancient ayatollah
wearing his *dulband*,
a shawl thrown across bent shoulders,
repeating Compline chants
after they have been sung,
"Let your holy angels dwell with us
to preserve us in peace,"*
the small bell of her voice lingering...

They named a new lavender garden
in honor of her fidelity
because she is a rapt gardener,
a flower in the midst of austerity,
fervently fringing stony soil.

Inside the chapel,
she sits in the chair ahead of me,
and I resist placing my hands
on her narrow shoulders,
wanting to enfold this small sparrow,

capture the spark of faith
that sees the unseen,
an imperishable presence
abiding like a newly-given morning.

I keep wondering
Did she ever belong to herself,
or has she just been a yield
of goodness to others?
rising each day from nightmare,
a rose recovered, smiling
in recollection of joy.

*From Compline, *The Book of Common Prayer*

II.

In the evenings, she enters a dark cell
but her soul is not asleep.

The nights are long,
and she often walks in her dreams,

believes the kitchen is still open,
makes coffee for herself and St. Benedict

who waits in the refectory, anxious
to voice a chronicle of complaints

about his monks who trespass The Rule
and claim a night of unbroken sleep.

She likes men, doesn't mind
if he spills coffee on a table set for breakfast,

desires to walk with him
through the invisible kingdom,

solemn eyes fixed on imagined cultivations,
roses in a garden that she knows

will not be rushing somewhere.

She invites the angels in
but they are heading home in the dark woods,

perceives someone knocking at the door,
breaking the dense silence,

wonders why the shutters are closed
against her memories, and dozes off

as the sun puts a finger to its lips,
letting the clock stop and night fall

on the narrow cot in an empty room.

ANGEL IN A SWING

The stone angel is laughing.
Gently anchored to a small swing

between aqua blue posts,
she sways in God's playground,

St. Mary's convent garden.

She can pump higher than twenty feet,
even swing sideways and touch

red and yellow blooms surrounding her,
a feat not approved by the Sisters

or their sedate God.

But she can attain the heavens any time,
spiraling high enough to leap

into the misty-laden air
and disappear into a funnel cloud,

if she wasn't already employed
to guard the souls

of the little Sisters in blue
who are sometimes frightened

by a wind jealous of constant prayer,
gusting out of the sharp bluff's

center of darkness,
and they do not wish to sail into the void.

THE SERENADE OF SISTER LUCY

No chords of Hildegard for her,
the key to sacred mysteries
was her acoustic guitar,
an altar of notes for playing Gospel
to the meanest heart, the easily lost,
a singing nun engaging the sorrowful
with a mountain tune.

Now, her guitar silent,
she plays no more late night gigs,
preaches from a wheelchair,
telling old stories about immortality,
having lived many lifetimes
filled with reliable hope,
years passing while something out there
tells her to stand firm
and listen to the lutes of angels.

Queen without a mantle
living in a fortress on the bluff,
she wheels her chair away
from the threshold of a long night,
listening to the music of rustling leaves,
her eyelids fluttering shut
during the chanting of Psalms,
lost in the deep shade of fading memories,
trying to let go of the longing.

ROCKING WITH HYMN 599*

It began like any other morning service
and ended in a crescendo of harmony,
hardly more than a dozen singing
on James Weldon Johnson's feast day,
melodious cries praising the One
who made us human,
blessed us with suppleness and strength
to lift up those who had escaped
subterfuge and spilled blood,
the marrow of bondage.

We sang "Lift Every Voice"*
in air charged with the question
"Who do you think
can hold God's people
when the Lord himself has said
Let my people go?"**
not a cracked note among us,
the sun coming through a side window,
an organist pumping out more light,
sounds of faith and triumph
drifting out the door,
shattering blood red rose petals
in a garden watered with ancient tears,
the broken bones of people of all colors
marching in to The Table,
clapping their wrinkled hands.

*Episcopal Hymnal
**Verses from *God's Trombone* by James Weldon Johnson

PENNY

Sister Madeleine Mary whose heart
lives in a secret room,
roams freely in the woods
following a dog the color of a roan
and of its namesake coin—Penny—
hardly an animal of lassitude
when roving with her mistress,
but one who sees Sister's visions,
shadows in the garden,
dark stairs leading heavenward,
joining her in the company of eternal time.

At Mass, she curls around herself
in a lined basket behind Sister's chair,
silent, a creature of ebbing faith,
dazed by the noise of chants,
opening one eye during the prayers,
bored by petitions and praise,
but showing exquisite behavior.

When storms swell on the bluff,
she cowers and whines at the frequency,
cannot sleep through the catastrophe
of a world thick with rain on dark leaves,
sees ghosts unexpectedly appear on the altar,
quivering, nudges Sister to shield her
and is given a coat
not unlike a strait jacket
to calm her raging fear
of the devil that rides outside.

She waits for her breakfast,
dog treats laced with Valerian?
dreaming of hearing a final bell
so she can get on with the hunt,
unafraid of blood on the snow,

can mangle some wily chipmunk
to lay at her mistress's feet,
quell Sister's visions of the great suffering,
her yearnings for the bliss of paradise.

SISTER ELIZABETH ON WINGED FEET

When she kneels on hard wood to pray
I see the thinning soles on her sandals,
worn treads of winged feet flying through
the Convent's silent halls all day,
climbing the stairs after Compline,
waking at night to fend off phantoms
haunting little Sister Mary Zita,
arising at dawn to make liturgical timetables,
to organize an army of Associates and Oblates,
her Hezekiahs of faith and prayer.

A smile betrays secret rapture
when she reads aloud the Old Testament,
as if she had practiced
the becoming of one divinely inspired,
a smile balancing the anger
because her feet have grown weary,
are not as winged as her spirit.
The caravan moves slowly,
there are too many rogue shepherds,
too much decline and compromise.

When I hear rain falling through leaves,
soft thuds on the roof
this sultry night in July,
I wonder if she ever embraces
the safety of the moment,
the present intensified,
not running toward an arrival
in the next strange city
to become known as an angel presence
carrying scrolls of past and future,
but alert to the first moment

rain flows into the Unconscious
at the threshold of sleep,
this stillness, an entry
into the sacred I Am...
the wisdom under the Word.

THE CONVENT CAT

You ponder the old nursery rhyme
with the picture of a sleeping cat,
a bright yellow beast on grey linen paper,
words warning: "if you don't hurt her,
she'll do you no harm,"
but there are no caveats
if Sophie harms you first,
shedding short bites of fur,
rubbing against your legs,
flaunting her sixth sense about allergies,
her perverse tiger nature,
licking her lips, twitching her nose
as you sneeze, blow your nose,
suffer a paroxysm of coughing.

The Sisters say she knows everything,
that you sit in a certain chair to pray
and when you are absent from chapel,
drapes herself in its seat, smiling, purring,
teaching you a lesson for missing the service.

She rubs herself into the seat of her day shift,
admiring herself in the mirror
of Sister Mary Martha's adoration,
demonic, her fur crawling with dander,
always giving you a polite smile
as her chaperone places her on a walker seat,
wheeling her into the refectory
to provide a healthy breakfast...
at your table.

The Sisters are proud of her superior insights,
daring you to step on her,
break through the magic circle
of their occupation,
and you burn a few candles,
asking the Lord to send her outdoors
where she can learn some refinements,
stay off of your chair of prayer,
or stay in bed all day in Sister's cell,
disappear down a rat hole.

It's a shame they think she's a believer,
strangely blissful about her immortality
when they speak of her nine incarnations,
a feline Madonna eying sparrows in the garden
or waiting for a mouse in the dark cellar,
scratching softly on a door that she knows...
will always let her in.

THE EAGER PSALM READERS

rush past the asterisk,
breathless with excitement,
reading about the wrath of the Lord
encouraging pilgrim feet,
as if the act of not pausing
would open the folded hands
of Canaanites worshipping idols.

Sister Madeleine Mary had to stop them,
they were reading without breathing,
bound to run into the mouth of wickedness,
swept adrift by succeeding lines of the Word,
trampling goodness underfoot.

Time out to reveal the heart,
speak what was right,
delight in the moon and stars,
blue smoke on the mountain,
wind in the valley,
rain on the cornfields,
to hear His powerful voice
speaking in slow, majestic tones...
breaking at the asterisk.

SISTER MADELEINE MARY PHOTOGRAPHS AN AMBULATORY

She weighed the scene in her mind
as if it were unwilling to make itself known,

a dark perspective, the covered walk,
splashes of gold glinting on its arches,

one pinpoint of light on closed doors at the end,
a place far from beckoning to lost travelers.

She saw herself floating through
a narrow channel, The Way,

prayer, the familiar buoy there.
Angels flew in the moonlight,

pointing out road signs,
and she walked straight into

doors without a porch light,
searching for the book

that held the names,
the archives of worthy nuns

who had slept through too many seasons,
sealed off from prying eyes

behind the heavy doors.

But she knew she could enter
for she had covered the distance,

had opened the shutter's eye
and captured The Way

in one ecstatic touch,
one flash of divine light.

THE CALL

In the room, a lamp without a bulb,
a cup of tepid water on the bedside table,

despair crouched in the corner
and all that was made came to me.

Lying abed, a recumbent form
reading Julian of Norwich's shewings,

a gift was placed in my hand
as it was placed in hers

during the agony of crossing over.

Julian clung to the idea of mercy,
telling us sin was meant to make us learn,

that we are not born evil,
that wrath is perversity

and suffering sent as a reminder
of The Passion dressed in different clothes.

O Lord, I said,
I am the ground of your beseeching,

turning her thought
you are the ground of my beseeching

inside out,
admitted I had eluded Him,

a frozen stream in sunlight,
passenger on a sidetracked train,

suddenly become a soul maker
in an old cathedral.

And from the bed,
for the sake of truth

I claimed the call
and all that is made,

arising to greet the sublime gaze
of the great I Am.

RETREAT AT THE HERMITAGE

A week at the Hermitage was long enough,
stone cottage on the bluff,

pot-bellied stove for tragic winters,
mattress on the bare floor,

space accommodating only two associates
steadfast in resolve to sedate

the restless mind and spirit,
witness to woods, the gray mountain,

Silence.

No television,
a radio playing Beethoven endlessly,

swaddled in prayer, reading
a book about Thomas Merton's life

I never finished,
the spirit of place informing me

I could never be a hermit,
desert mother, or a nun,

every stage of peace and renewal
leading to my return to carpets,

large beds, and upholstered armchairs
where there were no bells,

no hastening to Mass in a rock tower
four times daily,

chanting off-key at Evening Prayer.

It was no easy time,
the gray sky bending down,

a cold piece of cloth
I was unwilling to wear too long,

winds blustering on a bluff
I was unable to face,

lying in a few slats of light,
trying to make a reverie into meditation,

ready to exchange the sacred place
for roof, walls, wood of my home,

safe behind the familiar fence
of an everyday mystic.

THE MEDITATION GARDEN AT ST. MARY'S

Is there a hidden name to mark passage
into this looming stillness,
woods where he made a ring of stone,
God waiting above a kingdom of shadow?

The Magdalene women began walking
the meditations of sorrow,
stopping to pray for patience
under a pergoda made of rough logs,
a place of cross and shelter,
the listening trees urging new life,
soliloquies of mercy.

They planted lavender on the hill,
watering it with the miseries
of addiction, sexual abuse,
prostitution and incarceration,
their witness, an anguished heart,
love replanted on a hill no steeper
than the artless steps of the street,
the long walk where they lost
their lives in chains of darkness,

while God waited above a kingdom of shadow
in a meditation garden without a name,
temple of light riding on the wind
into a thicket of purple
just opening its eyes.

END TIMES

Now it is a place of sepulchral song,
age and illness in the pews
waiting for the final destination
when their blue skirts will whirl
in the blameless sky;
cautious because their rote prayers
belie a listless faith
and like their dog and cat
they doze in chapel,
missing the cues to lead the prayers,
bent double from the effort
of carrying one another's burdens,
unwilling to say it is finished,
but still honoring their namesake,
the *Virga mediatrix*
of the world, of the world
they cannot bring themselves to leave.

II

DIXIELAND AGAIN

Looking down at the yellow house,
I hope that some of Wolfe's poetry
will rise to my occasion,
drift through the dozen windows
fronting the walk,
but it is dark inside,
the only light that ever shone out
to the conflicted world
were the eyes in his massive head
bright as the yellow paint
on the house of his childhood,
the frame of his imagination.

Nine rocking chairs stand empty,
no audience on the gallery,
his sleeping porch faces the street,
reminders of tormented nights
when he moved from room to room,
forced by his mother's commerce,
an old boarding house
I have toured four times.

Each time I want his ghost
to give me a stone, a leaf, a door,
symbols in the torrent of words
wafting up three chimneys
and down the long walk,
echoes of his stories
landing in empty places,
emptier than the one he sprang from.

At midnight I again look down
at the orange glow of the porch light,
wondering why someone
placed the beacon there,
telling him he could come home again...
too late.

FAMILY BETRAYAL

Behind the scenes,
hate is sent by electronic speed,
the tribe holding their own court,
Bible in hand, joined as judge and jury,
deciding before she arrived
they would batter her with questions
because she dared question
The Way the Money Went...
in the Wrong Tone of Voice.

She received a sentence of paranoia
from the backwash of paranoid country,
a room heavy in shadow and secrecy,
muffled snickering, Judas kisses,
a grim exhibit of unity.
She tried to keep her eyes closed,
her mouth shut,
that was the way
in provincial southern towns
and family businesses where Family,
even if mad, superseded honest business.

Blood had better run thicker than reason,
they warned,
things ought to stay as they were
or she'd be in for a streak of bad luck.
If she wanted transparency,
tragedy hid in the bed
of a battered pick-up truck
that would take her out of town
leaving a trail of blood, driven over,
changed to nameless dust.

The mirror they now stand before
is a reflection of ruthless memories,
the buried inquisition,

fan blades turning relentlessly,
the shadow of a cross over her head,
a pale guillotine glinting on the porch.

But she departed. It was road's end.
Let the weeds grow over their graves.
Running in her body now,
a vein of pulsing freedom,
no more knives in the back
or endless hosing with cold water.
She had pronounced her own sentence:
no transparency:
no tribal allegiance.

All this, while someone in the background
strummed a guitar without strings.

IN NORTH CAROLINA, THE END IS NEAR

It's raining on the Jesus Saves billboard
shading the wild azaleas
where a forest of sugar maple and black locust
wave away transgressors,
travelers on No Name Road.

Mt. Hope Baptist Church
settles lower on the mountain
than an Episcopal chapel at 3200 feet,
large white scrapes appear
on red dirt slopes,
by elevation, the liberal bastion
looms a little closer to God's heart,
its fundamentalist neighbor
having fallen 1,000 feet
from grace.

Small streams tumble over rock
into quiet eddies near curves
veering dizzily at Bridal Veil Falls,
and just out of Highlands
in the sharpest curve,
the reluctant sun strikes
a message in uneven letters
nailed to a tree:
        REPENTANCE,
hidden prophets asking for renunciation,
a willow weeping at their feet,
doom trying to overtake the doubting traffic,
which knows there is more than this
within the tangled woods.

UPON VIEWING AN ENCAUSTIC PAINTING BY CONSTANCE WILLIAMS

We swim in the open sea,
gnarled outlines of moon shells,

organ and bone within a dream,
raised sludge forms

revealing contortions of the brain
from which we sprang.

And what are we?
How do we enter the doors

of narrow houses carved
at the bottom of the frame,

saved from solitary life?

They are the frames of places
where we have dared to come on land,

shapes pushing through to another world
to find holiness in everything

where the air is celestial green,
the ocean, a flickering light,

and the Infinite indulges his play impulse,
his spidery lines defining many lives,

the world we lived in,
the world we live in.

We will go on and on
despite the shadows whispering,

What are we doing here?
Why have we been summoned

to this provisional place,
this box of translucence on a wall?

THE SCENT OF NAHN

In the containment of rain
falling in these dense woods,
I think about parched plains,
a pallet of sandy earth suddenly watered,
Khuzestan province, January, 1974,
when rain fell all month
and the desert became a sea of mud.

I lived in the shadow of a storm,
a revolution that had not begun,
walking the streets of Ahwaz
as if I were on a movie set,
untroubled feet pacing in places
smelling of spices and dust,
looking for round ovens
tended by bare-chested men
dressed in cotton pajama pants,
not knowing it was a hurting place,
that their hunger was not appeased
by the warm wheel of nahn,
a flaky surface on which I spread
rich butter made in Holland,

I walked toward something
that would always be distant,
shuttered houses made of the mud
of an ancient country,
streets filled with shouting taxi drivers,
men squatting under a palm,
Farsi cries splintering the air
of a world reluctantly dry,
Muslim chants becoming ladders
of dissonant music.

I think of this broken place
as rain falls here and dust stirs
on the plains of Khuzestan,
an unrepentant desert that has lost its dreams,
forfeited its soul for this preying mantis,
The Arms Race.

I close my eyes and see black chadors
moving across the plains,
a caravan searching for twigs
of stunted trees,
beggars in a hot marketplace,
life, one colossal bazaar,
and I order a set of Farsi language tapes,
wondering if learning the language here
can be a camel carrying water
to parched throats there,
can redeem what I did not understand—
opposing latitudes, poles of dissent—
the sadness of those who told a different story.

A VISIT TO ANDALUSIA, HOME OF FLANNERY O'CONNOR

Did Flannery's mother call the farm "Andalusia" because the Spanish name means "The Land of the Most Holy Mary," or did she come upon Alabama's false interpretation of the name: "to walk easy," believing that the place would become comfortable and easy for her dying daughter? Surely, she wasn't taken with the name because Hank Williams married his Audrey at a filling station in Andalusia, Texas? But that incongruity could have been Flannery's wish for an unsuitable name—such characters lived in her stories about struggling beings. Was the name itself another one of her morality tales?

For Flannery, it was just a shady patch,
the screen porch on a hot, dusty road
where peacocks strutted their stuff,
spread their fans of many eyes,
watching her seize each day afresh,
live her life to the fullest
despite the useless legs that forced her
to lie on her back in the darkness of disease,
grieve the course of the bizarre world.

With words she possessed everything –
faith, love, tragedy entwined,
her destiny, to make the odd eloquent,
stained-paper people lurking in her study,
a crowd of unfinished beings.

For her, death was not the day the body died
but the night when language ceased

and her stories could no longer take flesh.
I think she preferred that the farm be called
"The Land of the Most Holy Mary,"
believing that by her devotion
she could induce Mary
to sit with her at the hour of death,
that the peacocks' voices were the ecstatic cries
of saints playing flutes, pulling her upward
on broken, useless wings,
leaving behind a final chapter of awe.

A DOGGED THOUGHT

Imploring, beseeching,
a dog's eyes,
the quintessential beggar,
glutton for affection,
doomed to speak
only the language
of his luminous eyes.

A creature who runs
after a stick,
because you throw it
to divert yourself,

comes out to greet you
even when treated
with mendacity,
waits on a corner
by the schoolyard
so you can fill
the empty bowl.

Sole resident
of all-day loneliness,
a solitary station
you chuff into,
claim as your companion
listening to the patter
of evening rain.

Gets up, shakes himself,
stares out the window
at the dead stars
of another life,

not judging how far
you are
from the single Truth,
Love.

Reads your thoughts
but says nothing
about the burden
of his own captivity.

Imploring, beseeching,
a creature reflecting
the nostalgia
of shepherd people
in his luminous eyes.

QUEEN ANNE'S LACE

Beyond the windows in a field of wild grass,
Queen Anne waves on a long stem,
her chaste white flowers a reminder
such innocence is kept
because her seeds are contraceptives,
as old a remedy as Hippocrates
who prescribed ingestion
after a night of heat
and a headlong moment
for better or worse.

A queen's name she bears,
royally loved by swallowtail butterflies,
fitting partners in noble dress,
poised above a dark purple floret,
the center of all that white lace,
telltale stain of dalliance.

She wears an alabaster dress,
fragile color in a field of yellow straw
where barns loom redder
against her white incursions,
bees doze in her sweet nectar
and humans dig her taproots...
all, attackers of refinement.

Yet she blooms and nods,
a blissful gift spreading her lace,
turning her head this way and that

to get a better view of the assault,
knowing when invaders gaze into the depths
of her guileless purple eye,
she will unrepentedly give everything away,
her heart always being with ours,
her eye opening in our mornings.

FOR FRED BEGUN

Performance: to present a dramatic or musical work
or other entertainment before an audience.

When I viewed a picture of Cybele,
Grecian earth goddess,
seated with tympanum
anchored on her left arm,
a lion nestling in her lap,
her body poised for drumming,
I thought of Begun,
master timpanist of the National Symphony,
a man who never played
a sitting down performance,
for us, the lion was his own leaping body,
a rapt movement in the air.

He could have performed
in a Dionysian rite,
absorbed in thundering sensation,
organizing sound that roared
into an altered state,
ecstasy in performer and listener,
taking to the air and coming down
on a triumphant beat.

They say his leaps into the air
narrowly missed the baton tips
of Copland, Stravinsky, Bernstein,
he was music's pulse, his thrumming
a bridge to synchronicity,
speaking for everyone.

Sinew and tendon tested
beyond marathon leaps,
he fell in the air
at each reverberation,
a percussion celebration
not unlike the rhythm
of black Gospel singing.
somehow following the score
but playing the music
according to how high
the instrument of his body could leap,
how far he could be swept away,
vibrating alpha waves,
poetry in motion.

Not allowed to open the curtain,
he closed it to a quivering audience
rising to its feet through the crash and rumble,
the dialect of a powerful drum
wide in range, large in spirit
ushering in another seven days of Creation,
despair and dream in every beat.

DREAMSONG

I dreamed I heard footsteps in the hall
and struggled to emerge from the dream

but slipped further into its hold.
I was searching for sheet music,

compositions for a B-flat clarinet,
my aunt's old Conn I never mastered,

noodling a lonely wail
that began the journey

of telling a life story in tremolos,
coaxing tunes through a split reed.

In the dream, I walked in and out of stores,
recognized a vague outline,

Main street in the town of my birth,
entered a hardware store

where the old bishop who ordained me
led me to a table of tinware,

dusty sheet music spilling over pots and pans,
and I paid $20 for notes I could not read.

This, I thought, is dying,
staying forever caught

in an undercurrent of musical metaphors,
the hold of one night's dream.

Although I could not read the music,
was unable to play the notes,

I felt inexplicable joy
when I saw large white creatures

fingering tin clarinets in meditative rapture,
playing unrehearsed arabesques,

recompense in a brilliant world of sound.

III

PERIPATETIC

Wandering,
always turning a corner,
exiting,
climbing blue ridges,
North Carolina, Virginia,
everything rising in plain view
while an invisible hand
guides us through heavy rain,
windshield wipers dancing,
taking us over the next hill,
the next exit
where someone is waiting
to show us around,
a festival, a fair, an art show,
places to eat the next meal.

The soul always in deep flight,
hearts skipping about
like wrens out of nest.
We grow wings in midsummer,
escaping heat in dark hotels
on upper floors,
rooms that smell of mold
and secrets,
in daylight wandering side streets,
seeking a remote world
and matters of little importance
time, our companion,
a stranger beckoning us

to a door we weren't looking for
into a shop displaying
hundreds of bottles of olive oil
bearing the imprimatur of a dove,
glowing with the yellow light
of a lamp left burning
on the night table...at home.

THERE ARE RIVERS YOU CROSS AND NEVER SEE

when you take a route up the Interstate
where concrete abutments are built
to protect drivers who lust for speed,
structures more important to civilization
than the view of water coursing alongside
congested highways, crowded Kentucky woods.

Are the rivers wide
or closed in by encroaching trees,
murky brown as Louisiana bayous,
or clear as the stream of the Bogue Chitto
at its unpolluted zenith
when you could see through
to pebbled bottoms and perch beds?
Can someone on these unknown riverbanks
see the sky reflected in their depths
or torrents of white froth cresting on rapids?

You unbuckle the seatbelt,
straining to sit tall,
to overcome the gray wall,
but fall back into the no-scenery of Interstate,
wondering if the abutment is an obstacle
or a way of warning you
not to look over the edge
into the purple dusk of the future.
Travel is reduced to a center line,
no veering off route
into rough waters of strange rivers.

You just watch the clouds float
and the world within your head,
stopping in unknown places
to ask about rivers you cannot see,

questioning people who never cross them
in a car on a busy highway,
who stay on the narrow path—
the weather of dry land—
afraid of curiosity and crossings,
who point toward something
called *never been there,*
then turn back into overgrown foliage...
and their sheltered eddies.

YARD SALE NEAR SPARTA, TENNESSEE

It could have been any county
following the downturn of 2008,

when all hopes began to center
on the sale of faded Bermuda shorts

and Grand Ole Opry t-shirts,
towels with no fluff,

tattered pillowcases,
ruby colored glasses from Quaker Oats boxes,

old Royal typewriters with sticky keys,
empty Jim Beam bottles and Crown Royal bags,

the detritus of families become dependent
on the battered wares in overgrown yards.

It was evidence of horoscope predictions gone awry,
passing fancies laid out on trestle tables,

an orphanage of discards in a landscape of want,
tables springing up everywhere like hillside toadstools

holding all they had.

Rain falls on this impoverished mural,
a downpour drenching the 25 cents table—

yesterday's yellow underclothing—
a wet display exposing bottom sizes

as revealing as a man running naked
through a dying cornfield.

A sad figure holding a black umbrella
shakes his fist at the sky,

wind moaning over the sound of rain,
water pouring into a zinc tub

filled with peeling tennis shoes,
and he is forced to take all of it indoors,

past an empty bed lying in shadow,
into the kitchen with a leaking roof

where children, dry as the picked bones
of a chicken they haven't devoured,

stand peering at his armload of trash,
pointing toward the blue painted shelves

of an empty cupboard.

IN A DULCIMER SHOP, BEREA, KENTUCKY

Wherever I go, whenever I confess
I was born in Louisiana,
someone takes up an instrument
and begins to make Cajun music.
In the hills of Tennessee or Kentucky,
Appalachian dulcimers, sound boxes
spanning over two centuries
pluck songs out of the swamp country,
reaching back to oak branches
and meandering bayous,
fingers moving swiftly
to escape from silence,
whamadiddles making notes on the wind,
sounds that tilt boundaries,
moving us in the same direction
toward endless prairie,
haunted swamp, gaunt mountains,
reaching out to pass a good time,
sobbing sweetly "Goodbye Joe,"
no matter the state.
These are the strains of bright angels,
boats rowing toward dawn,
birds carrying us into
the inevitability of God,
fingers pressing down
on the tunes of all our years,
even the bitter poems of injustice,
playing their way out of night,
the songs of endless births.

RUGBY, TENNESSEE,

a place of empty places...
twelve restored buildings line the highway,
evidences of a failed Utopian village
where Sam Wilson stayed on as postmaster,
vowed that the secret to his happiness
was his bachelorhood, a state protected
by a long flowing beard,
never shaved, never married,
photographed wearing suspenders and brogans,
homely and lonely-looking,
as desolate as I would have been
living in a sparse village
on the tableland plateau,
as forlorn as Miss Betty at dusk,
sitting before a fire she built herself,
smoking a corncob pipe,
hatchet visible under her bed—
symbol of some unknown legend
about one who preferred a virginal existence.

Listening to the sawing sound of katydids,
I imagine a life that would have made me
slow to get out of bed in the morning,
everyday a desultory Sunday afternoon,
nothing to do except check rain gauges,
the air thick with silence,
a path worn through to the spring.
I would have felt myself growing as old
as the roots of white oaks surrounding log houses
hemmed in by picket fences,

natural beauty and promise,
but as lonesome as cracked headstones
in a country cemetery filled with typhoid victims
who somehow thought they'd live like gentry,

if only the Cincinnati Southern Railway
had built a spur line to the town,
if only someone had cleared
enough old growth timber and tilled the soil,
instead of sitting on the veranda,
waiting for a good evening breeze,
writing a letter about "enchanted solitude."*

*Letter of Thomas Hughes, founder of Utopian Rugby, extolling the virtues of his utopian experiment.

EAVESDROPPING ON A WRITER'S CONFERENCE

She remained seated at a table,
replacement for the tall podium

because she was short in height,
certainly not in literary stature,

an accomplished teller of tales
but a cynical American whose half year in Paris

inspired wry observations about American life,
reading in soft, controlled diction

the blazing lines she had written
about marginalized blacks being lone sufferers

in God-blessed America.

And why are we here, she asked,
while it goes on and on over there?

Going on about our failures,
localizing pain to Europe, the Mideast,

any other country except the soil
on which she stood, uttering words

that would have shocked Auden.*

How many smoking towers in New York City
mock the Lady of Liberty in the harbor?

How many bombs in Boston
or shooters in Sandy Hook,

my ten-year old grandson
suffering with juvenile rheumatoid arthritis,

my daughter's panic attacks,
rampant child abuse and neglect,

gang rapes and kidnapped children,
Iraq veterans with maimed limbs?

Was there some quantifier in her statement?

How many rolling heads, broken hearts,
lonely afternoons, bees in a chimney, failed crops,

dead pets, sadsacks on bar stools
constitute universal suffering?

And through whose pain was she nurtured?
Was she an only child in a nefarious world,

forbidden to speak out
until she learned to write?

Surely she must have been missing a few chapters
in her well-written books,

now declaring that God-blessed Americans
have escaped human suffering

to a group of aspiring writers who know better,
or, perhaps, unlike most of her audience,

she has written away the pain,
is now leading a charmed life in a province

somewhere else in her head.

*W.H. Auden, author of "Musee des Beaux Arts," an ekphrastic poem which describes a moment of indifference to suffering.

FOR THOSE WHO HAVE GONE BEFORE

Archaeologists discovered ash heaps,
English halls that housed the dead,
circa 4,000 B.C.,
halls the grieving had burned to the ground,
mounding their ashes to form connections
between the living and the dead,
people who feared they were not infinite,
hoping that burial mounds
would help them know their families
had gone away to an unknown god
but stayed with them forever,
linked by the ashes of love.

Strange how they entered the gates
blinded and prone, as we all do,
moving past sentries who had no compassion,
who had rather not have let them in,
no one's life having lived up to the shoulders
of what they were supposed to do
with the gift of free will.

No matter the prayers
for the end of their time,
saints days, flowers on the grave,
they remain strangers
in an endless procession
of ashes to ashes, dust to dust,
excavation to excavation
of their brief season
in the dark grass of the world,
having gone as far as they could go.

YARD NOTES
I. SLUGS

Two nights of rain on the roof
and this morning I swept away slugs

encamped on the wet porch,
tawny-colored slime bodies

looking for a place to hide
from the few toads in our yard

and ducks paddling in a small pond
across the way;

hermaphroditic creatures,
self-fertilizing themselves,

each one leaving 500 eggs
to hatch under my porch.

During the evening porch talk
a small one drags slime underfoot,

angry that I have swept away
in the pools of water –

its siblings, legless, boneless cousins

who grate relentlessly
on the remains of a struggling garden

while I sleep
and the warm rain falls,

leaves shattered by strange migrants
toiling in the night soil,

inflicting plants with wounds
that will never heal,

and I settle into dreams,
reminded that nothing on this earth

belongs to us.

II. BROTHER RABBIT

Brown rabbit stares
through a bedroom window
while I dress,
calculating distance,
standing at the better point
of leaping away—outdoors—
as we watch,
enclosed in House,
outraged at his boldness,
not grunting or lunging,
eating around the edges
of our good humor.

Smug in his fur,
he acts as if he knows
his pelts are no longer fashion,
there's no need for frontier stews
in black kettles;
so he sits, nose twitching,
iron statue in the dew,
thinking, perhaps,
if moles can continue their work
tunneling our lawn,
why can't he mate
under the hemlock,
keep a leg up without apology,
breed in damp needles,
have a fleeting summer affair
ending in the birth
of blind and hairless offspring?
his Korean cousins making romance
and rice cakes on the moon.

III. NOCTURNE FOR A HEMLOCK

Foresters call it a "superlative,"
the 100-foot hemlock tree,
a green cathedral pyramiding
in my backyard,
now threatened by the hemlock wooly,
but the traffic I observe
underneath its lower branches
tells me it does not have declining health;
I have seen rabbits, coons, skunks, red foxes
emerge from underneath its crown
and wonder if it isn't an all-night tavern
where creatures make music,
dance, act out plays on a makeshift stage,
having a desire for entertainment
and happiness not unlike ours,
animals that come out of hiding at dawn
wearing carnival masks,
weaving in the bright beam
of the lighted parking lot,
passing out of view when the world is quiet,
the hemlock keeping their secrets.
A serious matter,
these forest dwellers with nightly passions,
although I sidestep their backrooms,
unwilling to take a look
into the tangled undergrowth
for fear one of them is still there,
leaning on the bar, singing
"Show me the way to go home,"
and I will have to oblige.

IV. SUMMER BATHS

Two stone bowls on pedestals,
"artificial puddles" devoid of water
except when filled by torrential rain,
reproach us about today's heat,
and the complaining cardinals and crows
who once plumped themselves
in our shallow bowls,
now nod on the outstretched arms
of an oak nearby.

We have allowed algae to line
the bottoms of carved basins,
to become slippery perches for aging crows,
although we once enjoyed birds in the yard
who doused their feathers,
welcomed Saturday night baths–
an abandoned memory of coolness.

They need a caring person to draw their bath,
someone like Grandmother Nell
who dunked Grandfather Paul
in the claw-footed tub
every Saturday afternoon,
scrubbing him with a brush
and a large bar of orange Lifebuoy,
threatening to drown him
if he didn't better his daily hygiene.

Now we invite birds for brief landings,
sympathize with commuting friends,
but reason that if we filled the slippery basin
rooted perilously close
to the tavern under the hemlock,

it would be like inviting them to die.
With no free and open foliage nearby,

our visitor might be stripped of plumage,
a gray cat emerging from beneath the tree,
smirks like a wicked Cheshire,
prancing near the smallest bath,

warning us it's better to welcome
a crow with drooping feathers
for a brief and dry dip
than it is to bury a dead one
who has lingered too long in the shade,
better to post a sign:
"For décor, not dipping,"
that only crows could read and understand,
bypassing us and flying
toward flowing streams in an unknown distance
where someone else has filled the bowl.

V. KATYDIDS
1.

Birds have vanished
from a night of breeding katydids,
their monotonous songs crescendoing
in the white oaks,
the noise breaking down limbs
that shudder and fall
on the grass of a shattered night.

They are waiting in the tree tops
for a mate to answer their call,
sawing songs in anticipation,
in daylight flattening oval-shaped wings
where predators roam,
emulating the living leaves
while they seek seeds and the ugly slugs
that plague my front porch,

green knights and princesses
that sleep on the old bedding of bushes
when light comes;
parents who don't take care
of the offspring soon to be born,
shun social groups,
have no consort with humans,
seldom seen, always heard,
cacophony in the darkness.

Behind windows I try to see them
standing on the stairs of tree trunks

with their green lights dimmed,
the air dense with songs about loving,
as if afraid of losing each other,
echoing and echoing repetitious lyrics
in a long heartbeat,
refusing to be suddenly hushed.

2.

Perhaps they are imitating
the monophonic lines of Hildegard,
seeking the attention of the Speechless One,
chanting in endless prayer,
beseeching Him who gave us song
to regain his voice, yet knowing
He expects us to speak for Him
over and over again
as they do... in love.

ABOUT THE AUTHOR

Diane Marquart Moore is a poet living in Sewanee, Tennessee during the summer and in New Iberia, Louisiana during the winter. She also writes novels, articles, and non-fiction books and has been an editor and a retired archdeacon of the Episcopal Diocese of Western Louisiana. Diane has lived in Louisiana, Texas, Maine, Tennessee, and in southern Iran during the reign of the Shahanshah. She writes a weekly blog entitled "A Words Worth." Her books can be ordered online or from borderpress@gmail.com or by mail from Border Press, P. O. Box 3124, Sewanee, Tennessee, 37375.

Made in the USA
Columbia, SC
04 March 2018